Ju
222
W14   Waldman, Sarah.
         Light: the first seven
days.

Temple Israel Library
Minneapolis, Minn.

———

Please sign your full name on the above card.

Return books promptly to the Library or Temple Office.

Fines will be charged for overdue books or for damage or loss of same.

Harcourt Brace Jovanovich, Publishers

SAN DIEGO   NEW YORK   LONDON

LIGHT

THE FIRST SEVEN DAYS

Retold by Sarah Waldman

Illustrated by Neil Waldman

Text copyright © 1993 by Harcourt Brace Jovanovich, Inc.
Illustrations copyright © 1993 by Neil Waldman

All rights reserved. No part of this publication may be
reproduced or transmitted in any form or by any means,
electronic or mechanical, including photocopy, recording,
or any information storage and retrieval system,
without permission in writing from the publisher.

Requests for permission to make copies of
any part of the work should be mailed to:
Permissions Department,
Harcourt Brace Jovanovich, Publishers,
8th Floor, Orlando, Florida 32887.

Library of Congress Cataloging-in-Publication Data
Waldman, Sarah.
Light: the first seven days/retold by Sarah Waldman;
Illustrated by Neil Waldman. — 1st ed.
p.   cm.
Summary: A retelling of the story of
creation from the book of Genesis.
ISBN 0-15-220870-4
1. Creation—Biblical teaching—Juvenile literature.
[1. Creation. 2. Bible stories—O.T.]
I. Waldman, Neil, ill.
II. Title.
BS651.W243   1993
222'.1109505—dc20   92-8767

First edition
A B C D E

The illustrations in this book were done in acrylic
paint on 140-lb. Arches cold-press watercolor paper.
The display type and text type were set in Albertus by
HBJ Photocomposition Center, San Diego, California.
Color separations by Bright Arts, Ltd., Singapore
Printed and bound by Tien Wah Press, Singapore
Production supervision by Warren Wallerstein and Ginger Boyer
Designed by Michael Farmer

To my mother,
who first gave me crayons and paper
and told me to write a book
—S.W.

For Sarah and Jono

My beloved, blessed children
are the flowers of a garden
in which I have grown.
The sweetness of their petals
has filled many of my days,
their glorious colors
exploding in sparkling radiance
and blessing my widened eyes.
Through the long winter
of my silence,
their blossoming
opened my heart
and gave wings
to my voice.
Their very being
is a blessing—
a wondrous blessing
that has graced my days.

—N.W.

ONCE UPON A TIME, before God shaped Heaven and Earth, the world was unformed and covered by a great sea. Darkness surrounded the waves.

And God said, Let there be light.
And there was light, and it was
good. The light was called
day, and the darkness, night.
And there was evening,
and there was morning,
the first day.

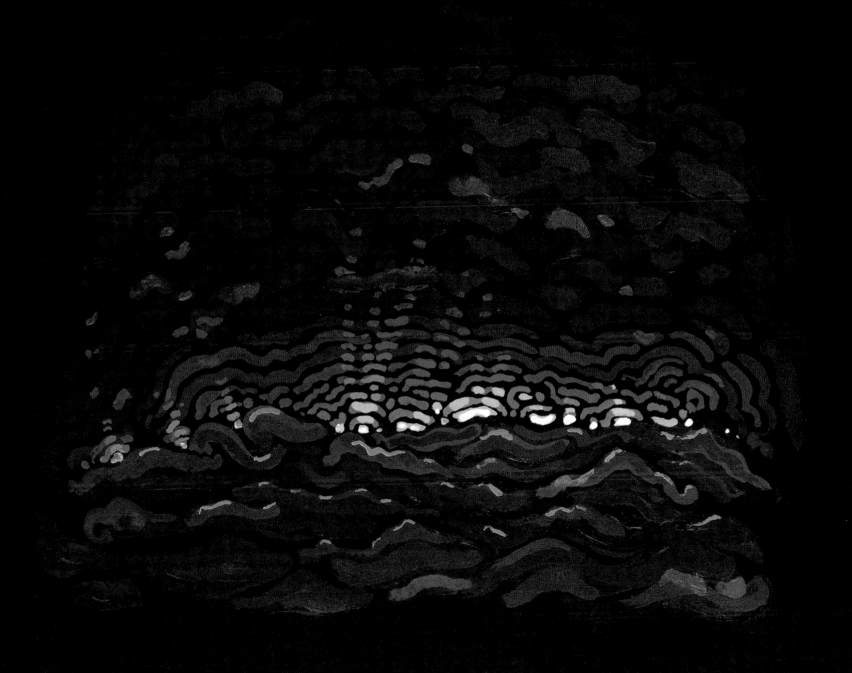

Then God made a sky above the waters. The sky was called the heavens, and it was good. And there was evening, and there was morning, the second day.

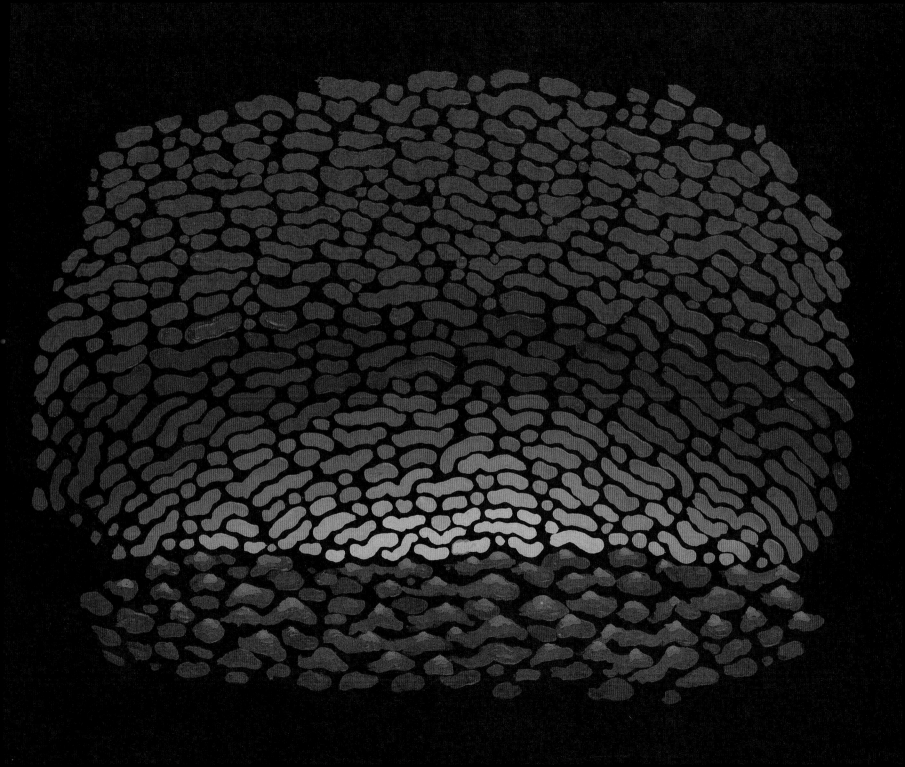

Then all the waters were
gathered into one place
so that dry land appeared.
The land was called earth,
and the waters, seas.

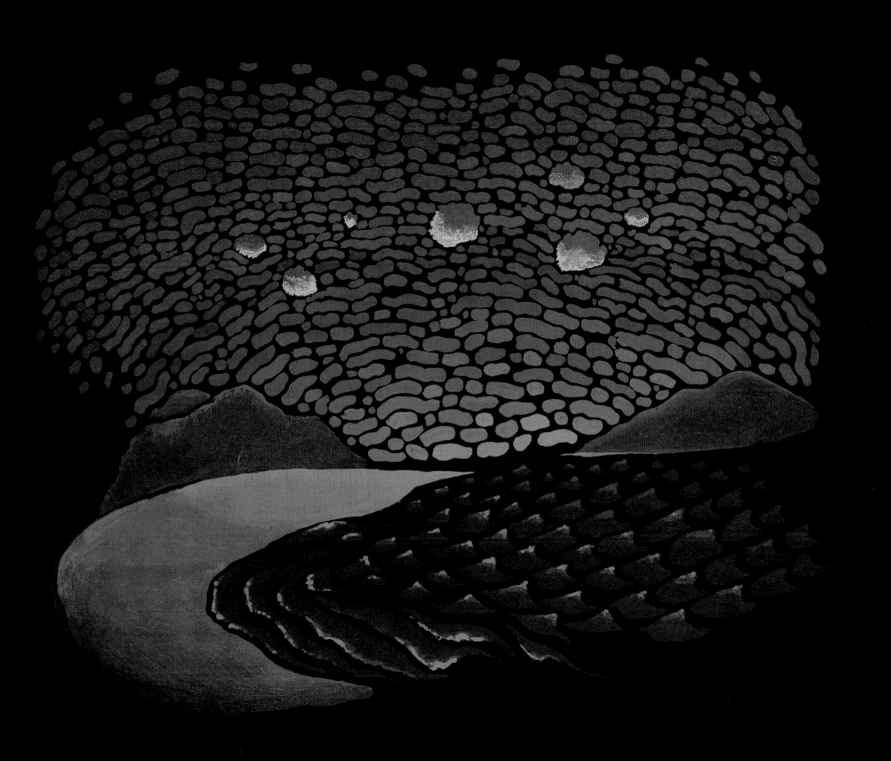

Then God said, Upon the
earth many kinds of plants
will grow: grasses and vegetables
and trees that bear fruit.
It was all very good.
And there was evening,
and there was morning,
the third day.

God made two great lights in the sky to brighten the days and the nights. These lights would mark the months, the days, the seasons, and the years.

The brighter light of the sun
would shine through the days,
and the softer light of the moon
would shine through the nights,
with the help of twinkling stars.
And there was evening,
and there was morning,
the fourth day.

And God said,
Let fish appear in the seas,
and birds in the skies.

And the fish and birds
were fruitful, and soon the
seas and the skies were
brimming with life.
And there was evening,
and there was morning,
the fifth day.

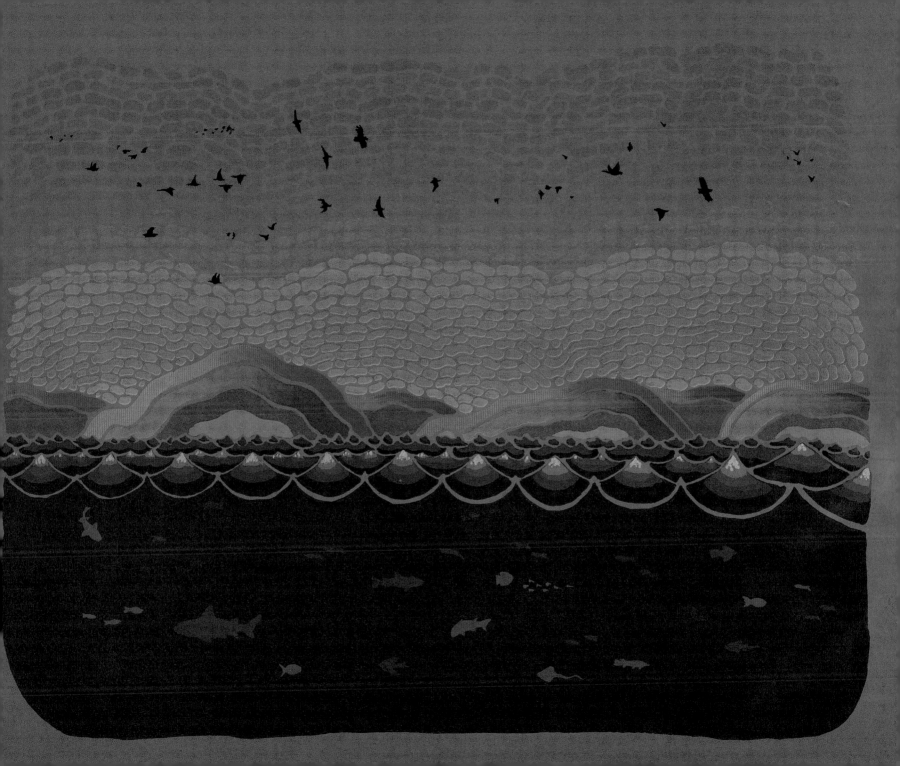

And God said, Let all kinds of animals appear upon the earth. And many creatures, great and small, appeared, and it was good.

Then God said, I will make people in my image. They will rule over the fish in the seas, the birds in the skies, and the animals on the earth. God made a man and a woman and told them, Have many children so the world will be filled with people.

The man and woman were given the grasses and fruit trees, fish, birds, and land animals. And God looked upon the newborn earth, and it was good. And there was evening, and there was morning, the sixth day.

Heaven and Earth and all
that were within them
were now complete.
On the seventh day God
stopped work and rested.
And this day became
a day of rest forever.

TEMPLE ISRAEL LIBRARY

STORYTELLER'S NOTE

People around the world tell stories about how the earth was formed; one widely known version is found in the book of Genesis.

Although there are differences, Judaism, Christianity, and Islam share the underlying concept of this creation story: The world was created in six spans or days. During this time, the sky and earth were separated and everything between was formed, the sun and moon appeared, day and night came to pass, and Adam and Eve took their first breaths.

The story of creation reminds people what an incredible place the earth really is. It helps us to remember to take care of our beautiful planet because it is a very special gift.

—S.W.

Temple Israel

Minneapolis, Minnesota

IN HONOR OF THE ANNIVERSARY OF

TED & CELIA DESNICK

FROM

ROSE SCHLEIFF